BRIGHT
IDEA
BOOKS

WEREWOLVES

by Marie Pearson

Raintree is an imprint of Capstone Global Library Limited, a company incorporated in England and Wales having its registered office at 264 Banbury Road, Oxford, OX2 7DY – Registered company number: 6695582

www.raintree.co.uk
myorders@raintree.co.uk

Edited by Claire Vanden Branden
Designed by Becky Daum
Original illustrations © Capstone Global Library Limited 2021
Production by Colleen McLaren
Originated by Capstone Global Library Ltd

978 1 4747 8770 3 (hardback)
978 1 4747 8780 2 (paperback)

British Library Cataloguing in Publication Data
A full catalogue record for this book is available from the British Library.

Acknowledgements
We would like to thank the following for permission to reproduce photographs: Alamy: Chronicle, 14–15, 17, The Natural History Museum, 23; iStockphoto: duncan1890, 11, hkuchera, 26–27, 29, Johny87, 12–13, ortlemma, cover, rudall30, 31, station96, 6–7, ysbrandcosijn, 19, 28; Newscom: Album/British Library, 20–21; Hartmann Schedel/The Nuremberg Chronicle/akg-images, 9; North Wind Picture Archives: 5; Shutterstock Images: Joe Seer, 24–25. Design Elements: Shutterstock Images, Red Line Editorial.

Every effort has been made to contact copyright holders of material reproduced in this book. Any omissions will be rectified in subsequent printings if notice is given to the publisher.

All the internet addresses (URLs) given in this book were valid at the time of going to press. However, due to the dynamic nature of the internet, some addresses may have changed, or sites may have changed or ceased to exist since publication. While the author and publisher regret any inconvenience this may cause readers, no responsibility for any such changes can be accepted by either the author or the publisher.

Printed and bound in India

CONTENTS

CHAPTER 1

A WEREWOLF Tale

Norse people once told a scary tale. A father and son found two men. They were covered with wolf skins. There was a **spell** on the skins. The skins fell off every 10 days. Then they were people again. But the skins would grow back.

The father and son took the shed
wolf skins. They put them on. Then they
turned into wolves. The pair ran through
the woods. They killed many people.

**Norse people passed
on tales through
a storyteller.**

5

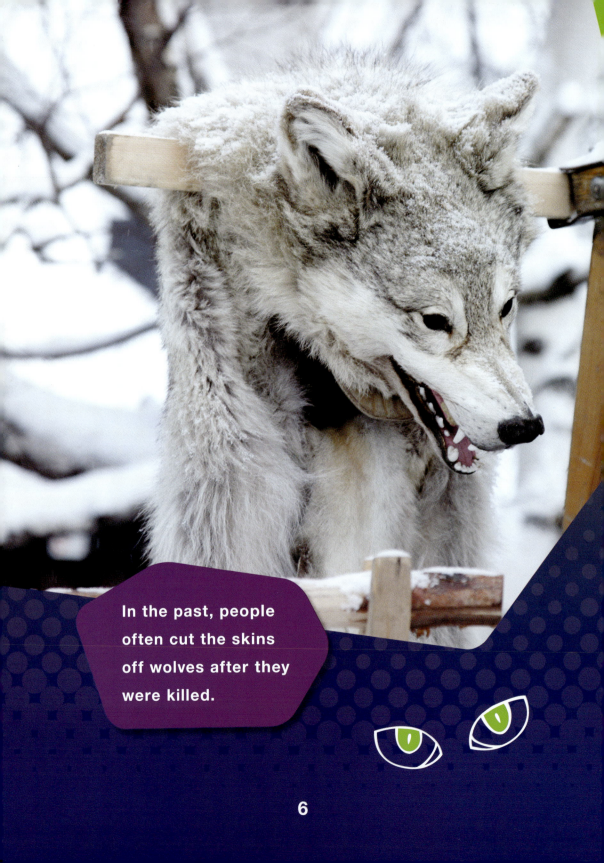

In the past, people often cut the skins off wolves after they were killed.

One day the father and son fought. The father bit the son in the throat. The son almost died. But a bird dropped a magic leaf nearby. The father put the leaf on the son's throat. It saved his life.

Then the father and son shed their wolf skins. They decided to burn them. They would never become wolves again.

This werewolf story was told in the AD 1200s. A werewolf is a person who can change into a wolf. People have told werewolf stories for hundreds of years. Many still find these stories scary today.

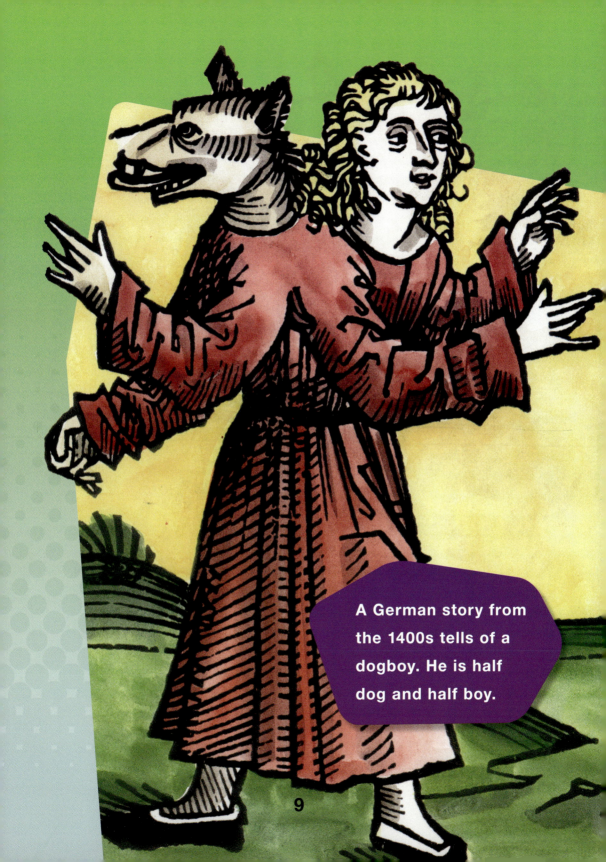

A German story from the 1400s tells of a dogboy. He is half dog and half boy.

9

CHAPTER 2

DEATHS IN France

People in France once thought werewolves were real. This was mostly during the 1500s. Many men were **accused** of being werewolves. It was said they had made a deal with the **devil**. It was a crime to be a werewolf. They were put to death.

Men who were accused of being werewolves were often burned at the stake. At the time it was thought to be one of the only ways to kill a werewolf.

Stories of werewolves spread. One man said he was attacked by a wolf. He fought back and hurt it. The wolf got away. But the man followed it. He said it led him to a house. A man called Michael Verdun lived there.

Wolves are strong creatures that can kill animals much larger than themselves. This made people terrified of werewolves.

The man saw Verdun. He was hurt in the same place as the wolf. Verdun was arrested for being a werewolf.

Many people were afraid of werewolves during the 1500s and 1600s.

Verdun was **tortured** for days. Finally he said he was a werewolf. He may have said it to end the pain. People today know he was just a person.

TIGERS OR BEARS

Some places do not have wolves. Stories in these areas tell of people turning into tigers or bears.

CHAPTER 3

MANY
Views

Only men became werewolves in the earliest stories. Tales today tell of women werewolves too.

In stories people become werewolves for many reasons. Sometimes they start as people. But then they do something bad, so a god turns them into wolves. They may never be human again.

In one story, the ancient Greek god Zeus turns a man called Lycaon into a werewolf.

CHANGING FORM

In other stories a werewolf bites someone. That person can then change back and forth. Sometimes they are a wolf. Sometimes they are a person. A full moon may cause the change. Others control the change themselves.

Some tales say a werewolf looks like a real wolf. In other stories they are bigger. Werewolves often have **fangs**. They have claws and hairy bodies. Some are a mix of a person and a wolf. They may walk on two legs.

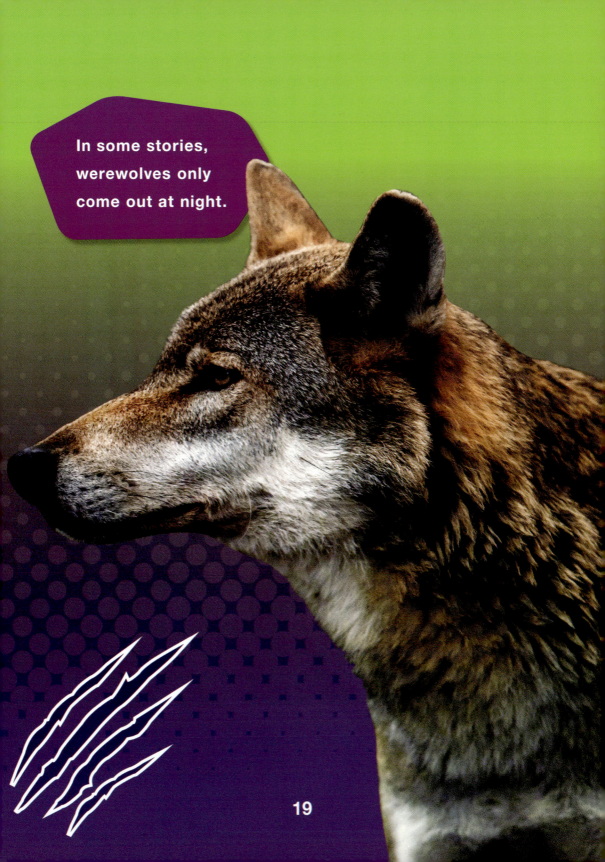

In some stories, werewolves only come out at night.

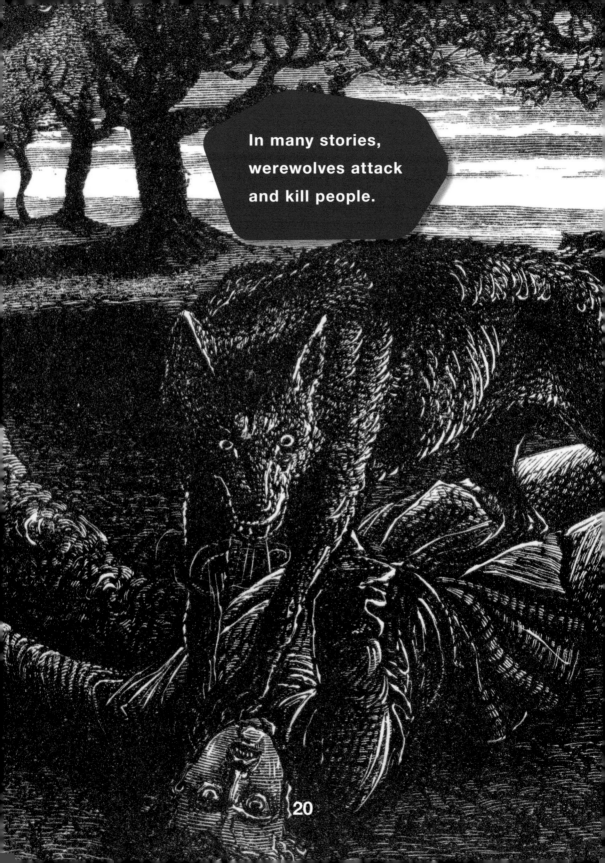

In many stories, werewolves attack and kill people.

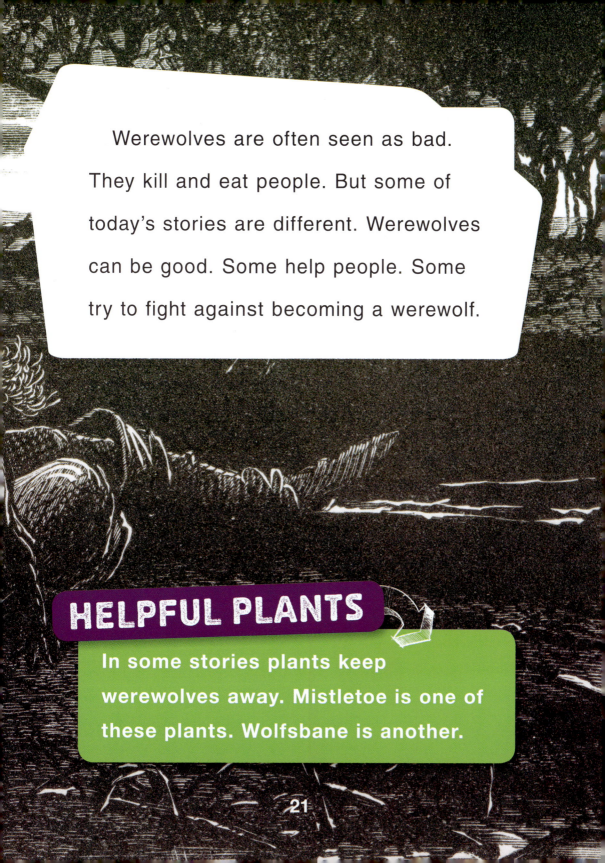

Werewolves are often seen as bad. They kill and eat people. But some of today's stories are different. Werewolves can be good. Some help people. Some try to fight against becoming a werewolf.

HELPFUL PLANTS

In some stories plants keep werewolves away. Mistletoe is one of these plants. Wolfsbane is another.

CHAPTER 4

WEREWOLVES Today

Many people once believed in werewolves. But there were reasons behind the belief. Some people had an illness. These people grew extra hair. Others who saw this may have started some werewolf stories.

Over time people came to know that werewolves are not real. But some people still think they are. Werewolf sightings are reported every year.

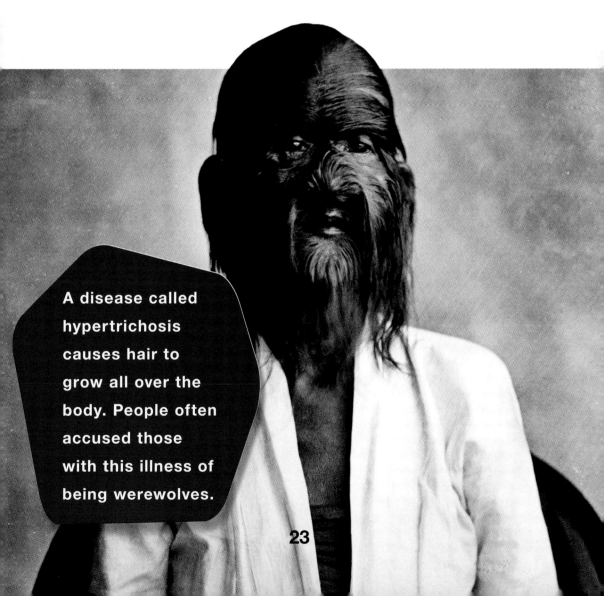

A disease called hypertrichosis causes hair to grow all over the body. People often accused those with this illness of being werewolves.

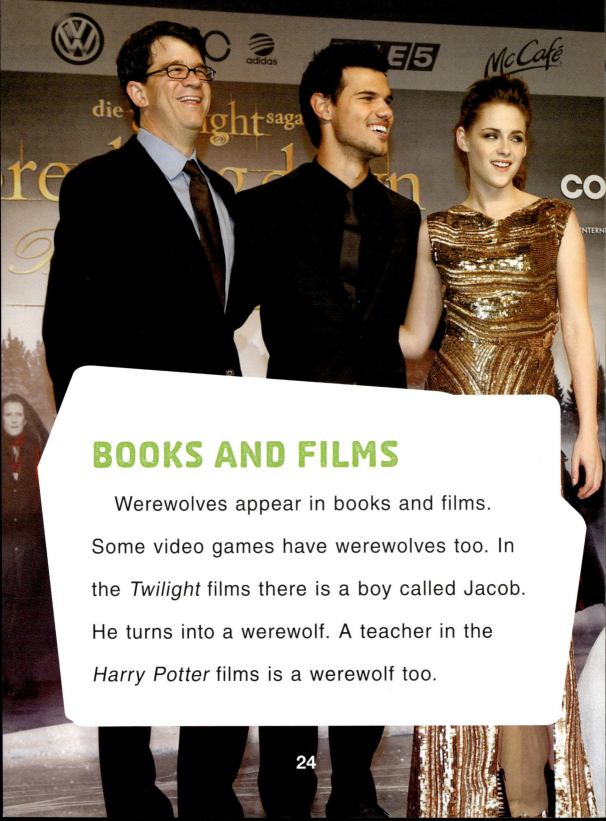

BOOKS AND FILMS

Werewolves appear in books and films. Some video games have werewolves too. In the *Twilight* films there is a boy called Jacob. He turns into a werewolf. A teacher in the *Harry Potter* films is a werewolf too.

In the *Twilight* films, Taylor Lautner (second from left) played the werewolf Jacob.

KILLING A WEREWOLF

In many films werewolves are hard to kill. A silver bullet is often the only way. *The Wolf Man* came out in 1941. The film made this idea popular.

Some writers use these monsters for fear. Werewolves have super speed. They are really strong. Most cannot control their need to kill.

People still enjoy stories of werewolves today. Some are scary. Some are filled with action. They make people ask what it means to be a person.

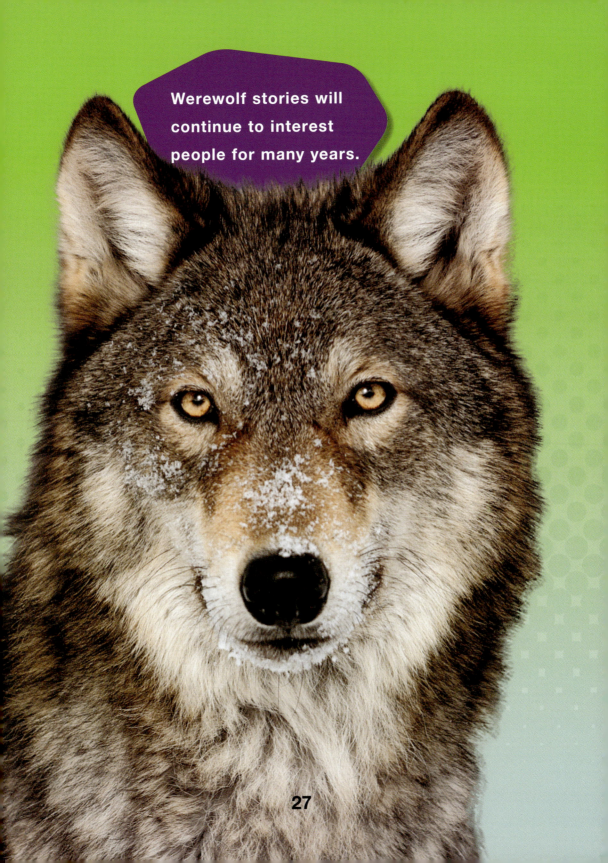

Werewolf stories will continue to interest people for many years.

27

GLOSSARY

accuse
say that someone did
something wrong

devil
evil spirit

fang
long, sharp tooth

Norse
people who lived in what
are now Norway, Sweden,
Denmark and Iceland

spell
words believed to have
magical powers

torture
cause extreme pain
to someone

TRIVIA

1. *The Epic of Gilgamesh* may be the oldest-known werewolf story. It was written in ancient Mesopotamia, in what is now southwestern Asia. The story was found on stone tablets from the 600s BC.

2. Lycanthropy is a condition in which people believe they can change into a wolf, even though they cannot.

3. Hypertrichosis is also called werewolf syndrome. The disease is very rare.

ACTIVITY

Think about how werewolves are described in this book. Now imagine you are designing a werewolf for a film. Sketch, sculpt or build a model of what it will look like. What do its head and neck look like? Does it look more human or more wolf-like? Write a few sentences explaining your choices.

FIND OUT MORE

Books

Children's Book of Mythical Beasts and Magical Monsters, DK
    (DK Children, 2015)

Norse Myths (Mythology Around the World), Eric Braun (Raintree, 2018)

Werewolves (Mythical Creatures), Rebecca Rissman (Raintree, 2011)

Werewolves and Vampires (Solving Mysteries with Science), Jane Bingham
    (Raintree, 2013)

Werewolves: The Truth Behind History's Scariest Shape-Shifters
    (Monster Handbooks), Sean McCollum (Raintree, 2016)

Websites

www.bbc.co.uk/bitesize/topics/zx339j6/articles/ztxwsrd
    What is a myth? Find out more!

www.bbc.co.uk/cbbc/quizzes/aotp-asian-mythology-quiz
    Which mythical creature are you? Take the quiz to find out!

INDEX